Pishi & Parents

Written by Dr. Samineh I Shaheem

Designed by Neda Shahzadeh

Grosvenor House
Publishing Limited

Round and round we go,
we will always be guided
by this glow!

This book is published by
Grosvenor House Publishing Ltd
Link House
140 The Broadway, Tolworth, Surrey, KT6 7HT.
www.grosvenorhousepublishing.co.uk

A CIP record for this book
is available from the British Library

ISBN 978-1-80381-024-9

Dedication

This book is dedicated to brightening children's lives by providing meaningful moments of valuable learning experiences. We help the most disadvantaged children around the world by donating a percentage of the proceeds of this book to various charities, with the aim of improving the lives of our most vulnerable and beloved members of society.

KINDNESS

"Carry out a random act of kindness, with no
expectation of reward, safe in the
knowledge that one day someone might do the
same for you."
Princess Diana

Kindness is one of the most important
attributes we can teach our children.
•It should be regularly practiced at home
and at school.
•Model kindness in your home by the way
you interact with each other, as well as
other family members and guests.
•Talk about ways we can all be kind by
telling your child stories of caring acts.

HELPING HAND

"If you want children to keep their feet
on the ground, put some responsibility on
their shoulders."
Abigail Van Buren

•Getting your children involved in household
chores will teach them important skills.
•Try different activities and see which ones
they are most interested in.
•Remember to let them keep trying until
they get it right. Quitting isn't an option!

GOOD HABITS

"You may delay, but time will not, and lost time is
never found again."
Benjamin Franklin

Constantly postponing or procrastinating when
it comes to doing chores does not form effective
future habits.
So what could you do?
•Have a structure.
•Set up a rewards system.
•Take away whatever might be distracting your child
from starting their chores.
• Never use chores as a form of punishment!

QUALITY TIME

"Family is not an important thing. It is everything."
Michael J. Fox

- The best gift we can give our children is the gift of quality time together.
- Toys and gifts will never take the place of the attention and affection of parents and care providers.
- Put your devices away and be fully present in these magical moments together.

MANAGING EMOTIONS

"No one cares how much you know, until they
know how much you care."
Theodore Roosevelt

•One of the most important qualities to have as a
parent is Emotional Intelligence.
•Emotional Intelligence allows us to communicate
calmly and effectively,
both in good and difficult times.
•Next time you're angry count to the magic
number, 6, and take a few deep breaths before
addressing the issue
by finding solutions.

VALUES AND DECISIONS

"You can only become truly accomplished at
something you love. Don't make money
your goal. Instead, pursue the things you love doing,
and then do them so well that
people can't take their eyes off you."
Maya Angelou

•There are lots of free activities that we can
do with our children.
•It's important to teach them the value of money
and making good decisions.
• You don't need to buy something every time
you go out!

MAGICAL MANNERS

"Respect for ourselves guides our morals,
respect for others guides our
manners."
Laurence Sterne

- Be consistent with the rules you set for
your children.
- Children need to learn patience as a part
of being polite.
- You are responsible for the way you shape their
behaviour and actions.
- Your children not only learn what you teach them,
but they also observe your behaviour, so try and
make sure there is an alignment between what you
say and what you
do!

ACKNOWLEDGEMENT

This book has been a collaborative effort between people who care about our present and future generations.
Thank you for being a part of this journey with us!

What

have

I learned

from this book?

Dr Samineh I Shaheem is a Dean and Executive Director, Professor of Business Psychology and Leadership, Learning & Development Consultant as well as Neuroleadership Coach. Every project holds importance and an opportunity to grow and advance, including one that had a significant positive impact on the UAE community; Dr Shaheem's Bolt Down on Bullying campaign started in 2010, where she set out to confront and prevent bullying. Dr Shaheem is an author, keynote and TEDx speaker with a successful track record in the design and delivery of culturally relevant, innovative courses and skill building programs. For the last 2 decades, she has worked across numerous industries and countries, including the US, Canada, the Netherlands, the United Arab Emirates and the UK.

Neda Shahzadeh has been passionate about creativity and art from childhood. Neda studied Fashion Design and Marketing in London before entering the world of luxury retail. She worked for Matches Fashion and many of the well-known brands, including Prada, Chanel and Lanvin. Inspired by the character 'Pishi' that her daughter Diba designed, she set off on a mission to create a series of educational books for kids and parents.

CPSIA information can be obtained
at www.ICGtesting.com
Printed in the USA
LVHW072056090622
720907LV00006B/98